Original title:
Tropical Whispers

Copyright © 2025 Creative Arts Management OÜ
All rights reserved.

Author: Lila Davenport
ISBN HARDBACK: 978-1-80581-584-6
ISBN PAPERBACK: 978-1-80581-111-4
ISBN EBOOK: 978-1-80581-584-6

Harbingers of the Morning Mist

Sunrise giggles, the sky wears a grin,
Parrots gossip, they're in a spin.
Coconuts dance on the feathery breeze,
While flip-flops plot to escape with ease.

Pineapple crowns on a lounge chair throne,
I swear they dance when left alone.
A crab with swagger, he struts his stuff,
In a world of shells, he thinks he's tough.

Enchanted Nights with Fireflies

Under the stars, the glowworms tease,
Who knew those bugs could move with such ease?
Laughter bubbles in the tropical night,
As coconuts join the moon's delight.

A lizard bursts in a tux, too fine,
While the beach ball dreams of being divine.
A conch shell 'crackles' just to catch a break,
Claiming the spotlight is no small feat to take.

The Soliloquy of Lapping Waves

Waves whisper secrets with every splash,
While sunbathers plot their sunburned bash.
Flip-flops squawk as they hop down the sand,
Guess they know this beach, oh so well planned!

Every nibble of fried fish makes them squeal,
As seagulls swoop in for a sneaky meal.
A catamaran chuckles at all the fuss,
Feeling quite proud in its floaty bus.

Tides of Memory in Salted Air

Shells hold tales in a salty embrace,
While seaweed wiggles in a slow-paced race.
A dolphin giggles, flips high and proud,
As beachgoers cheer and laugh aloud.

The sunburnt folks want everyone to see,
Their vibrant shades of red, a sight to be!
The wind plays tricks, swoops hats from the shore,
While a funny crab shimmies, begging for more.

Luminescent Moons Over Coral Reefs

The fish wear pajamas, they're swimming in style,
While crabs play the banjo, they dance for a while.
A jellyfish juggles with pearls and a shell,
Under moons that glow bright, oh can you not tell?

The starfish throw parties, with snacks made of sand,
They chat about ocean and tides so grand.
With bubbles as drinks, they make quite a scene,
In this waltz of the waves, they're kings and they're queens.

Conversations with the Coconut Trees

The coconuts gossip, they swing to and fro,
'Can you believe the wind? He's such a big blow!'
The parrots all squawk, sharing tales of their day,
As palm fronds tell secrets, they sway and they play.

'The sea turtle's slow,' one nut starts to jest,
'But he has the best shell; he's truly the guest!'
They chuckle together, in sunshine they grin,
As beach balls roll by, they sip on the wind.

Whispered Secrets in the Sand

The grains have confessions, like sand castles grand,
They giggle and wiggle, just under the hand.
A crab tells a secret, it's quite a tall tale,
Of beach bums and surfboards that float like a sail.

The seagulls drop hints, with feathers and flair,
Of picnics and laughter, and who stole the pear.
As waves break in rhythm, so lively, so spry,
The sand piles up dreams, like clouds in the sky.

Beneath the Mango Tree's Embrace

The mangoes hold meetings, they plot and they scheme,
'Let's make the fruit salad the ultimate dream!'
The monkeys all chatter, swinging with glee,
'Who'll throw in a banana? Now that's a great spree!'

The branches creak softly, like laughter and fun,
As the sun starts to dip, the day's almost done.
Together they giggle, in nature's embrace,
Underneath the bright leaves, it's the best kinda space.

Island Murmurs

Crabs in tiny suits do dance,
Under moonlight's playful glance.
Fish wear shades, oh what a sight,
Wiggling up for a late night bite.

Parrots squawk, a gossiping crew,
Passing secrets on ocean blue.
Coconuts roll, they giggle so loud,
As sea turtles wear hats feeling proud.

Secrets of the Palm Fronds

Leaves whisper tales of mischievous warmth,
Bamboo sways, keeping up the charm.
Lemurs share gossip, so suave and keen,
While monkeys toss coconuts, oh what a scene!

Dancing shadows in emerald shades,
Laughter echoes as sunlight fades.
All the critters join in the fun,
Planning mischief 'til the day is done.

The Swaying Breeze's Lullaby

Waves chuckle softly, tickling the shore,
While seabirds debate who's the biggest bore.
Sandcastles tumble, they laugh at the tide,
As seashells hold secrets they cannot confide.

Wind carries whispers of jellyfish pranks,
While octopuses draw colorful ranks.
With each little giggle, skies turn bright blue,
In a world full of wonders, where friendship is true.

Echoes from the Sunlit Shore

Flip-flops flip and catch a breeze,
As laughter dances among the trees.
Seagulls wear sunglasses and strike a pose,
While beach balls wobble in humorous rows.

Surfboards chat about the perfect wave,
Full of thrill, but none feel brave.
With each splash, a joyful cheer,
As beachgoers tell jokes that everyone hears.

Serenade of the Sunlit Leaves

The sun tickles the leaves so bright,
As lizards dance in pure delight.
Squirrels chuckle from their high throne,
While sipping juice from a coconut cone.

A parrot squawks a silly tease,
While monkeys swing like you and me.
Palm trees sway with joyful grace,
With a wink for the sun on their face.

Echoes of Paradise

A chubby toucan cracks a joke,
While turtles tease a nearby yolk.
Coconuts giggle as they roll,
Juggling seeds is their keen goal.

Light beams dance on the water's skin,
While fish below wear broad grins.
Raindrops leap and do a spin,
The jungle's laughter draws us in.

Murmurs in the Mango Grove

Mangoes whisper tales of cheer,
As butterflies flutter without fear.
A lazy bee hums a tune,
While a chameleon changes 'neath the moon.

Swaying vines play peek-a-boo,
A crab in the mud starts to woo.
The breeze carries a giggle or two,
As sunbeams dress the grove in dew.

Lush Shadows of the Rainforest

In the shade where shadows twist,
A sloth's slow dance can't be missed.
Frogs croak in a chorus weird,
Singing jokes that leave us cheered.

Under leaves, a spider grins,
As glitter bugs gather in spins.
Here laughter floats with every breeze,
Nature's antics aim to please.

Harmonies of Blooming Fields

In the fields where daisies dance,
Silly bees miss their chance,
Wiggly worms in line for a show,
Waving at flowers, all in a row.

Pineapples wearing a fruity crown,
Turnips trying to grow a frown,
Rabbits hop, making it clear,
They laugh at carrots, oh-so-near.

Sunflowers twist, showing their backs,
While daisies tease in colored packs,
Butterflies stumble, what a sight,
Chasing their dreams with all their might.

Breezes tickle every petal fair,
As garden gnomes start to dare,
Springtime's antics, a comical spree,
In a blooming world, just let it be.

Echoes of the Lost Sands

Footprints lost in a sandy maze,
Lizards posing in the sun's gaze,
Crabs join the dance, quite absurd,
Bouncing around, haven't heard a word.

Coconuts fall with a thud and roll,
Seagulls laugh, that's their goal,
Beach balls bouncing, chasing the tide,
While sunburned tourists take a ride.

Yet seaglass glimmers, a hidden treasure,
Bringing laughter, quite the pleasure,
Conversations of shells, all mixed in cheer,
Echoes of joy, they're always near.

Sandcastles crumble, yet spirits rise,
As shadows dance under bright blue skies,
A melody of giggles fills the air,
Nature's comedy, beyond compare.

The Kiss of the Coconut Wind

Coconuts rocking, a fruity parade,
Swaying to rhythms that never fade,
Palms gossiping in whispers low,
Tickling the breeze, putting on a show.

Bananas slip in a comical spin,
While monkeys crack jokes with a grin,
Tropical breezes dance through the trees,
Carrying laughter on a soft tease.

Frangipani petals float down like dreams,
As the sun paints the ocean in gleams,
Old tortoises chuckle, sharing tales,
Of wobbly walks and fantastical sails.

So let your cares get caught in the breeze,
Join in the fun, do as you please,
In this land where humor won't hide,
Feel the joy with the wind as your guide.

Fish Tales Beneath the Mangroves

Fish gathering round the old mangroves,
Trading tales only each one knows,
A puffer fish racing, puffed up with pride,
While a silly eel feels it should hide.

Shrimps in a jig, oh what a sight,
Twisting and turning, such pure delight,
Starfish snicker with arms in the air,
Inviting the crabs to join their fair.

Mudskippers hopping on slippery land,
Making fish faces as they stand,
"Look, I can walk!" one loudly squeaks,
While dolphins banter, trading techniques.

Bubbles arise from beneath the tide,
With jokes and laughter hiding inside,
In this underwater world of glee,
Fish tales thrive, wild and free.

Serenade of the Midnight Waves

Moonlight dances on the sea,
A crab boogies, wild and free.
Fish throw parties with a splash,
Seashells sing as they all clash.

Seagulls gossip, cawing loud,
While the starfish forms a crowd.
Jellyfish glow, a disco ball,
Waves roll in – it's quite the haul.

Driftwood drummers keep the beat,
As clams and oysters tap their feet.
Beach towels flutter, flags on high,
Even the sandpipers are spry.

Sneaky dolphins tease the shore,
Making waves, they want some more.
With laughter echoing through the night,
Midnight waves are pure delight.

Chasing Shadows Beneath the Canopy

Parrots squawk a joke or two,
While monkeys join the playtime crew.
Lizards bask on sunlit rocks,
Even vines tie funny knots!

A sloth slides down, quite a sight,
Grinning wide, it calls at night.
Hey, watch that leaf, it's quite the show,
Beneath the trees, we all just glow.

Snakes throw hissy fits of glee,
As beetles roll their bumble bee.
Frogs in chorus, ribbit and croak,
Their antics make the jungle choke.

Chasing shadows, laughter swirls,
Among the ferns, the fun unfurls.
In this leafy, laughing place,
Nature shows its wild, funny face.

Vibrant Dreams in the Jungle's Heart

Colors clash and critters leap,
In vibrant dreams while others sleep.
Butterflies flaunt, in fancy dress,
And dancing ants cause quite the mess.

A parrot tells ridiculous tales,
Of lost adventures and treasure trails.
Insects chirp with comedic flair,
While frogs breakdance without a care.

Coconuts tumble off their tree,
Claiming they're just wild and free.
Laughter echoes, bright and clear,
As jungle folks all gather near.

Vibrant dreams spin tales of cheer,
With every giggle, the night is near.
In the heart of this bustling scene,
Funny faces reign supreme.

The Rhythm of Rushing Waterfalls

Water splashes, creating beats,
Fishes dance with wiggly feets.
A monkey on a floating log,
 Jumps on in; it's just a fog!

Droplets tap like a light drum,
As turtles sway to the fun hum.
Nature's orchestra is at play,
In the waterfall's bubbly ballet.

Coconut hats fly overhead,
As critters snack on fresh-baked bread.
With every splash, they laugh aloud,
 Jokester fish join in the crowd.

A rainbow forms where laughter streams,
In the rhythm of joyful dreams.
Waterfalls bring joy and fun,
 Silly antics for everyone!

The Dance of the Hibiscus Blossom

Underneath the swaying tree,
A blossom twirled, so wild and free.
It danced with bees, a silly chase,
In nature's cuter, charming space.

The petals laughed, a giggly crew,
On breezes soft, they flew and flew.
With sun-kissed cheeks and dewy eyes,
They swayed like dancers in disguise.

A coconut chuckled nearby,
As mangoes rolled and tried to fly.
The sea breeze joined, a playful friend,
In this parade that had no end.

So if you hear a gentle song,
Remember blooms where they belong.
In every giggle, every sway,
Nature's joy is here to stay.

Swaying to the Island's Melody

Beneath the palms, the breezes tease,
While lizards shuffle, doing the freeze.
A parrot squawks, a comical sound,
As waves erupt and dance around.

Sand castles crumble with a plop,
As children giggle, never stop.
Coconuts roll like playful pets,
As island life forgets regrets.

With laughter shared, they sway and twirl,
The island spins, a joyful whirl.
Each shift of breeze brings smiles anew,
In this quirky ballet, all is true.

So join the fun, just like a song,
Where every moment feels so long.
In harmony, we find our beat,
The island's rhythm—life's sweet treat.

Petals Adrift in Sunset Light

As day gives way to twilight's charm,
The petals dance without alarm.
In colors bright, they laugh and glide,
In sunset's warmth, they take a ride.

A flower's wish floats on a breeze,
To meet the stars and swim at ease.
It twirls around with giggly cheer,
And wishes on the moon so near.

The twilight giggles, softly so,
As shadows play a game, you know.
Like fireflies in a game of catch,
Each spark a smile, with none to match.

So when the day draws to a close,
Remember petals and their prose.
In every swirl, there's joy to fill,
As sunset whispers, laughter's thrill.

Afterglow of a Rainy Afternoon

As raindrops giggled on the ground,
The flowers swayed without a sound.
They wore their hats of dew and mist,
In puddle-jumps, they can't resist.

The frogs grinned wide, in chorus sang,
While colors brightened with a bang!
Each splash released a giggling cheer,
As sunbeams danced and drew so near.

The world turned vibrant, painted bright,
Where colors blended, pure delight.
With every stroke, a painter's dream,
An afternoon, with laughter's theme.

So next time rain begins to fall,
Just open wide and have a ball.
For in each drop, a joke is spun,
In joyless weather, let's have fun!

The Enchantment of Distant Shores

Sandcastles rise, then wane,
Seagulls dance like wild trains.
A crab wearing a hat, oh my!
Who knew crabs were so spry?

The sun, a lazy, golden sphere,
Makes sunburns happen, I fear.
A splash! A laugh! A frantic chase,
As jellyfish join the race!

Waves clap hands, a tuneful roar,
While beach balls roll to shore.
In the distance, a dog does bark,
But he's searching for his spark!

Oh, how we jump and twirl with glee,
Laughter ringing like a jubilee.
Each wave a joke, each breeze a friend,
This silly journey has no end!

Crumbling Stone and Grassy Isles

Old rocks chuckle, cracks and all,
With stories of the sea's great brawl.
Grass writes poems in the breeze,
Whispering jokes through swaying trees.

Lizards leap in silly ways,
Imitating dance from yesterday.
A turtle wearing funky shades,
Struts along in bright parades!

The canoes bob, like they're alive,
As folks try hard to take a dive.
But splashes fly like confetti spreads,
While dolphins giggle in their beds.

Here, each rock has a sense of fun,
Even the clouds play hide and run.
In the green, wild laughter calls,
It's a place where joy enthralls!

The Scent of Rain on Dry Soil

A pitter-patter on the ground,
The dance of droplets makes a sound.
Earth drinks up with giddy glee,
As ants rejoice in jubilee!

Worms pop up like little springs,
Eager for the rain that sings.
A puddle splashes, laughing loud,
As kids jump in, proud and clouded.

The sun peeks through, what a tease,
Leading to rainbows with such ease.
Clouds wear hats while basking bright,
A comedy of weather in sight!

The scent so sweet, a joke afloat,
As nature sings in playful coat.
This playful dance with sky and soil,
Reminds us all how dreams uncoil!

Taste of the Island's Sweet Air

The breeze is sweet, a playful tease,
Tangoing with beautiful trees.
Once in a while, a parrot calls,
With jokes that bounce off sandy walls.

Coconuts roll, hilarious sight,
As they plot to take off in flight.
Mangoes wink from branches high,
Teasing the folks who pass them by.

Each wave whispers in joyful code,
Cracking jokes on the marine road.
Breezes chuckle, tickling your hair,
In this realm of sweet, salty air.

So come and dance where laughter thrives,
In the land where joy arrives.
With each breath, you taste the mirth,
In this wild, giggling earth!

Paintings in the Mist of Dawn

The sun peeks through, a cheeky grin,
While fish in pajamas begin to swim.
Chasing shadows, a monkey swings,
On branches where laughter forever clings.

Birds wear hats in the morning air,
A parade of colors, none can compare.
The coconut falls, a comic surprise,
As it rolls down the hill, oh how time flies!

Sandy toes and playful waves,
The sea makes jokes, our spirit it craves.
With laughter echoing, we dance on the shore,
In this silly world, who could ask for more?

Every dawn's brushstroke paints a smile,
Where worries vanish, even for a while.
So let's toast to mornings that sparkle and play,
For each comic wave brings a brand new day!

Lost Treasures of the Coral Reef

In the depths where the fish all wear bling,
A treasure chest sings, 'Come, see what I bring!'
Crabs in tuxedos are having a ball,
While jellyfish waltz, they wiggle and crawl.

The octopus juggles seaweed and shells,
While clownfish whisper, 'Do you hear the bells?'
A starfish giggles with five-pointed grace,
As seahorses ride in a merry chase.

Coral castles with windows of glass,
The best underwater cabaret, so sass!
With laughter and bubbles, we dive and we twirl,
In this whimsical world where weirdness can whirl.

Lost treasures are found in each twist and turn,
From goofy angles, we laugh and we yearn.
So let's raise a fin to this merry spree,
For the reef's silly antics are pure jubilee!

Songs of the Moonlit Shore

Under the moon, the beach comes alive,
The crickets chirp, while stars take a dive.
A sea turtle dons a hat, oh so round,
As sandcastles sway to the music's sweet sound.

With seagulls in shades, they strut down the lane,
Belting out tunes, as if in a chain.
The tide takes a bow, not wanting to part,
In this concert of waves, pure joy fills the heart.

Fireflies twinkle, they're the back-up band,
While the wind tells a joke, how clever and grand!
Each crash of the wave adds a beat to the night,
A silly serenade, oh what a delight!

So let the moon smile, cheeky and bright,
Guiding our laughter into the night.
For in each little song, with a wink and a cheer,
We find joy in the moments, forever held dear!

Secrets Shared with the Wind

The breeze carries whispers of laughter and glee,
As palm trees gossip, 'Come dance with me!'
A squirrel in a bow tie, so dapper and neat,
Displays his acrobatics, oh what a feat!

The wind tells of travels it's had on the sea,
Of seashells and wonders, and shenanigans free.
From silly old pirates who couldn't find gold,
To mermaids who giggle, oh tales to be told!

Clouds play peek-a-boo, with the sun as their friend,
While kites laugh aloud, on a whimsical bend.
The world spins in color, no worries to bind,
As secrets of laughter are shared with the wind.

So twirl with the gusts, let your spirit take flight,
In this funny dance, all your cares out of sight.
For the breeze knows the joy of the lives that it's found,
In the merriment shared, let our laughter resound!

Karst Mountains Hold Their Secrets

Up high the rocks do chatter,
Their mysteries in the breeze;
A curious goat gets a free patter,
While birds giggle among the trees.

Clouds wiggle, stretching their seams,
As if they're hiding their fate;
A lizard slips, bursting our dreams,
With a jump that seals his date.

The limestone grins, showing its age,
Wearing cracks like a wise old sage;
Each whisper of wind turns the page,
In the tales of this rugged stage.

Yet down below, the tourists fumble,
Tripping on roots while they stumble;
With the mountains watching, they tumble,
Like an awkward dance, oh how they grumble!

The Dance of Flamboyant Blossoms

Petals twirl in colors bright,
As bees laugh and take their flight;
They bump and bounce, what a sight,
A floral ballet, pure delight.

Sunshine winks, throwing a fit,
While daisies flaunt, enjoying the skit;
Laughter bursts from every bit,
As nature joins in with a spit.

The orchids flip like cheeky clowns,
As tulips wear their royal crowns;
With every gust, off come the gowns,
In this garden, there are no frowns!

So join the fun, the flowers insist,
For every visitor can't resist;
With petals swirling in joyous mist,
Who can say they don't feel blissed?

Notes from the Salt-Kissed Air

Whispers frolic through ocean spray,
They tease the seagulls on their way;
Shells giggle as the kids play,
While crabs throw shade, what a dismay!

Jellyfish jive in the sunlight,
With tentacles waving, oh what a sight;
They dance gracefully, oh what a fright,
While beachgoers scream, "Not tonight!"

The breeze croons soft lullabies,
As mermaids peek with twinkling eyes;
They chuckle as waves play tricks and lie,
Leaving behind the sand's surprise.

So take a breath of this salty tune,
As the sun dips down, oh so soon;
Every laugh echoes under the moon,
In the symphony of the afternoon.

Lush Melodies of a Forgotten Beach

The waves hum songs of days gone by,
Where flip-flops squeak and seagulls fly;
Old driftwood chuckles, oh my,
As sand crabs dance, oh me, oh my!

The tide rushes in, slips on a shoe,
It trips and giggles, what a view;
Shells chime in, joined by a crew,
On this stage, a frothy tableau.

Bananas sway, hanging on trees,
As monkeys swing without a tease;
They poke their heads, laughing in breeze,
Making mischief as sweet as cheese.

So let's recline on this sandy bed,
With laughter ringing, no room for dread;
In this forgotten dream where all's been said,
Life is a beach, just follow the thread!

The Lure of Hidden Coves

In a cove where the sun likes to play,
Crabs dance like they own the café.
Shells chatter secrets with ocean's delight,
Fish play tag, oh what a sight!

Mangoes drop like silly bombs,
While the parrots laugh and give out charms.
You'd think the coconuts share wise advice,
But they just giggle, quite precise!

Hammocks swing with an aching groan,
Every nap feels like a throne.
Yet in dreams, the waves plot and scheme,
To toss us all into their dream!

So join the noise of nature's crew,
With laughter painting skies so blue.
For every cove whispers a tale,
Of mischief and joy that will never pale.

Mystic Sounds of the Rainforest

In the rainforest where the frogs croak loud,
Trees wear coats, they are so proud.
Monkeys swing with a whoop and a wave,
To see them dance, oh, we'd all rave!

Leaves gossip under the rain's sweet kiss,
While the toucans laugh, what pure bliss!
The sloths, in slow motion, always confused,
"Did I eat this, or was it bruised?"

Every rustle tells a silly jest,
While the ants organize a tiny fest.
The beat of drums made from bark so dry,
"Join the party, don't be shy!"

So wander here with a grin so wide,
In the rainforest, where fun can't hide.
The sounds are mystic, but don't you fret,
For silliness reigns, the best duet!

Melody of the Ocean's Breath

Waves clap their hands on the sandy shore,
Like excited friends, they shout for more.
The dolphins in a flip flop parade,
Stealing the show, they can't evade!

Seashells gossip, whispering sweet,
"Is that a crab with dancing feet?"
Starfish lounge in their stylish attire,
"Who needs to hurry? We'll never tire!"

Surfers chase the waves like a game,
Each wipeout just adds to their fame.
Mermaids giggle with shimmering tails,
As the sea breeze carries their tales.

So come dip your toes where the sea plays,
Laugh along as it splashes and sways.
In this melody of ocean's breath,
There's no worry of fun's sweet death!

Reflections on Serene Waters

In calm waters, the ducks wear crowns,
Floating like kings, ignoring frowns.
The lilies bloom with a fragrant chat,
"Did you see that frog? Such a prankster brat!"

Ripples laugh as they dance around,
While the fish boast of treasure found.
A turtle slides with the grace of a pro,
In this sleepy realm, time moves slow.

Sunset paints the sky with a giggle,
While the heron strikes a pose and a wiggle.
"Just another day in our water ballet,"
Nature's circus puts on quite a display!

So float along, let worries drift,
In serene waters, life is a gift.
Each reflection holds a playful tease,
In this realm of wonder and breezy ease.

Celestial Dances of Fireflies

In the dark, they twinkle bright,
Like tiny stars taking flight.
They wobble, they giggle with glee,
Who knew bugs could dance like me?

They flash a signal, oh so slick,
A bug's disco – with a flick!
I tried to join, tripped on a leaf,
Now I'm the joke, what can I believe?

While they buzz around, having fun,
I ponder if I'm the only one,
Crickets chuckle, a chorus so sweet,
Just don't ask me to find my feet!

As they flit through the nightly haze,
I chase shadows for a while, in a daze.
Next time, I'll just sit and cheer,
Dancing's for bugs; I'll have my beer!

Ghosts of the Marine Sunset

Beneath the glow of the setting sun,
Fish in costumes, oh what fun!
A fish in a hat, another in shoes,
Giggling as waves sing the blues.

The crabs wear shades, looking all cool,
Aquatic antics, they rule the pool.
"Watch out!" I shout, as I slip on a shell,
They just laugh; guess it's a "sea shell" spell!

With jellyfish floating like sad balloons,
They sway with the rhythm to underwater tunes.
Starfish twirl, trying to impress,
While I bob my head in a glittery dress!

But the moon rises, they all disappear,
Leaving whispers of laughter I hear.
Tomorrow, I swear, I'll join their spree,
But tonight, I'll nap with the seaweed glee!

Colorful Life in the Lagoon's Depths

Down below in waters bright,
A parade of colors, a wondrous sight!
Fish named Bob and a clown with flair,
Practicing jokes in a seaweed chair.

An octopus juggling with eight arms wide,
Shrimp in tuxedos, they shimmy with pride.
They flash their fins, oh what a crew,
Underwater giggles, just for a few!

Crabs rolling by on their backs, oh dear,
"Why walk when you can glide, my dear?"
They toss sea stars, catching a laugh,
A slippery, silly mathematician's graph!

In the lagoon, where laughter takes flight,
Fish wearing tuxes swim away at night.
But I'll be back for the next big jest,
With bubbles and joy, we'll have a fest!

The Languages of the Exotic Birds

In the trees, they chatter away,
Funky feathers, bright as the day.
"Polly wants a cracker?" quips one with a grin,
While the others just laugh and dive right in.

The toucan's beak is a sight so bold,
Telling stories of adventures untold.
An owl hoots jokes, wise and sly,
While mockingbirds mimic, oh my oh my!

A parrot insists he's the best of the lot,
With ruffled pride, he struts on the spot.
"I'm bilingual, can't you see?"
As the nearby squirrel rolls his eyes with glee.

As twilight falls, they sing a song,
A cacophony; it won't take long.
While I sit back, catching their quirks,
In this feathered circus, life just works!

Ephemeral Beauty of the Blooming Seasons

Butterflies dance, quite a sight,
Chasing petals in the sunlight.
The daisies giggle, do they bloom?
Cacti blush, adding to the room.

Lizards skitter, dressed in green,
Pondering what the flowers mean.
A bee trips over, what a fail!
On sweet nectar, it leaves a trail.

Clouds drift by, like cotton candy,
Sunshine spills, isn't it dandy?
Squirrels debate on the best pine,
Thoughts of snacks, oh how they pine.

In this garden, laughs collide,
Nature's whimsy, pure and wide.
Each bloom a joke, a playful tease,
Life's a giggle beneath the trees.

The Enigma of the Deep Blue

Fish play tag in the azure sea,
Wave after wave, what glee to see!
A crab trips over its own claw,
It shrugs and struts, a real faux pas.

Seagulls squawk, the comedians here,
Scooping snacks, oh dear, oh dear!
Dolphins leap, with flair they shine,
Then belly flop, such a fine line.

Shells tell tales, if you pause and listen,
Who knew it held such odd ambition?
Octopus jests inky refrains,
Trying hard to hide, yet remains.

The tide retreats with a cheeky grin,
Leaving jokes in foam, where to begin?
Laughter bubbles in depths so deep,
In this watery world, secrets keep.

Selkie Songs and Island Echoes

Waves are laughing, brimming with cheer,
Selkies frolic, never a fear.
They shed their skins, like coats so fine,
Teasing the sea with a splash, divine.

Clams whisper secrets, so bold and rare,
While crabs hold court in seaside fair.
A seal begins to sing a tune,
Chasing shadows beneath the moon.

Sailors giggle at tales long spun,
Of mermaids and fish in the setting sun.
Seaweed wigs sway, with style and grace,
In every ripple, a smiling face.

Echoes of joy in the breezy air,
Every breeze a tickling dare.
Island life, a revue so wild,
With salty laughter, nature's child.

Fragments of a Verdant Eden

Leaves chatter softly, a gossiping spree,
In this patch of green, laughter's the key.
A frog croaks jokes, has the loudest voice,
Even the flowers can't help but rejoice.

The breeze bursts in, a playful breeze,
Twirling the ferns with elegant ease.
A squirrel steals nuts, what a cheeky heist,
But then trips on roots, oh, is this nice?

Ants hold parties, marching in lines,
Worms groove beneath, wriggling in twines.
Sunshine sprinkles golden delight,
As nature chuckles in morning light.

Mushrooms parade in polka dot hats,
Underneath branches, the banter chats.
In this slice of paradise, laughter swells,
Every corner a story, each whisper tells.

The Gravity of an Ocean Embrace

A seagull swoops in, takes my snack,
I chase him down, but he won't track.
With weighless grace, the waves come in,
Yet they slip away, just like my kin.

The sand sticks tight, as if bewitched,
My flip-flops gone, I feel quite ditched.
The tide then pulls, a sneaky grip,
I tumble forward, take a dip!

My friends all laugh, loud and clear,
As I emerge, all wet, I cheer.
Embraced by salt, my hair's a fright,
Who knew ocean love could be so light?

With fishy breath and seaweed strands,
I dance with dolphins, make new plans.
But in this realm of giggles and play,
There's never a dull, wave-tossed day!

Illuminated Paths through Verdant Vines

The leaves they rustle with every prank,
A monkey steals my drink; oh dear, I sank.
I chase him through the emerald maze,
In daylight's glow, I'm lost in a haze.

Beneath a fruit tree, I stumble and trip,
A burst of laughter from the nearest zip.
The sunbeams dance like they know my name,
In this leafy world, it's all a game.

The vines entwine like friends at a fest,
I wish to rest, but I'm far from blessed.
Through twirling paths, I post a plea,
For a map, a compass, or just plain tea.

The evening falls, bugs buzz around,
I'm plastered in petals from head to ground.
Among the greens, I realize with glee,
Nature's jokes are the best, for free!

The Journey of a Wandering Tide

The sea rolls in, a mischievous tide,
It tosses my chair, my snacks, and my pride.
Sailing along on a float too small,
Dodging an octopus's slippery squall.

A jellyfish waves with jiggling grace,
Wants to join my sunbathing space.
With laughter shared, a splashy reply,
This tide, I swear, has a sense of sly!

I drift and swerve, like a boat in a breeze,
But then I spot a crab, oh what a tease!
With claws a-clicking, he taps my arm,
"Don't drift too far, it's all charm and harm!"

So here I float, in a whimsical plight,
In tidal mischief, morning to night.
With salty kisses and sun-kissed arms,
Every wave whispers its endless charms.

Reverberations of Exotic Nights

The beach party starts with a bang and a bump,
A conga line forms, I trip on the lump.
With ukuleles strummed under the moon's glow,
I wave my hands like I'm in a show.

Coconuts cheer with drinks so fruity,
A dance-off begins, oh how it's hoot-y!
My feet get tangled, I spin, I twirl,
Join the laughter, let the fun unfurl.

With lanterns swaying, the ocean hums,
While unaware of our clumsy drums.
Stars overhead blink, amused by the sight,
Of me trying to dance in semi-dark light.

As dawn edges in, we sigh with delight,
These nights so wacky are always just right.
The echoes of joy, like a sweet serenade,
In this paradise, we'll never fade.

Driftwood Tales of the Forgotten Coves

Once a piece of wood did roam,
Caught a crab and made it home.
Told the tales of storms and tides,
While the gulls cracked jokes with pride.

Drifted past a starfish's chair,
It grumbled loud, 'Life isn't fair!'
Every wave would roll on by,
As the driftwood waved goodbye.

Met a turtle with a hat,
Said, 'Time to dance, now imagine that!'
So they twirled on the sandy shore,
With a conch shell band, they begged for more!

Whispers of the wind would tease,
While the seashells chuckled with ease.
Oh, the fun in salty spray,
As the driftwood danced the day away!

The Oracle of the Island Breeze

In the shade where palm leaves sway,
An oracle had much to say.
Gossiping with the honeybee,
Claimed it could predict my tea!

Coconut crabs debated loud,
Whether they should join the crowd.
Visions that made even nets giggle,
Future wrapped up in a wiggle.

The breeze blew through with cheeky flair,
Tossing hats into the air.
Whispers of secrets, giggly sighs,
Chasing away old, long-lost lies.

With each forecast like sweet delight,
It said, 'You'll dance with fish tonight!'
Island secrets made the sun beam,
Just don't forget to pause and dream!

Celestial Dances on Leafy Floors

Underneath the stars so bright,
Leaves would twirl in pure delight.
A monkey spun with joy so true,
And blamed it all on a mango stew.

Fireflies gathered in a line,
Said, 'Let's put on a show divine!'
With twinkling lights and flashes bold,
The night's dance floor turned to gold.

Frogs croaked out their finest tune,
While crickets tapped their feet in June.
Even owls hooted, 'What a sight!'
As they swayed throughout the night.

So if you hear this laughter play,
Just know the woods invite you to stay.
For under the sky that twirls and glows,
We dance together, where mischief grows.

Murmurings of an Island Dreamscape

In the morning, waves would pout,
While dreaming seagulls flapped about.
'What's for breakfast?' they would ask,
'A crab or two, that's our task!'

By the dock, a fish did frown,
Claiming it had missed the town.
Life beneath was such a bore,
It craved a picnic on the shore.

Whispers of the mango trees,
Told of stories in the breeze.
Jellyfish laughed at passing boats,
While watching them with cheeky notes.

So in this land of vivid dreams,
Nothing is quite as it seems.
Join the fun, let laughter sing,
In the world where smiles take wing!

The Call of Distant Shores

Seagulls squawk, the crabs do dance,
Palm trees sway in a sandy trance.
Flip-flops flop, the sun's a tease,
Lemonade spills with every breeze.

Beachball bobbles, laughter soars,
Sunscreen battles against the roars.
Flip a fish, catch the sun,
Who knew that fun could weigh a ton?

Shells are treasures, says the lore,
But they just scoff and roll onshore.
A starfish poses, striking a pose,
"Smile for the 'Gram!" — as everybody knows.

So grab a chair, and take a seat,
On sand that feels like a warm treat.
Crack a joke, sip a drink,
Life's too short; let's not overthink!

Rhythms of the Island Heartbeat

Drums beat steady, feet begin to sway,
Coconuts spill; they're here to play.
A hula twist sends giggles wide,
Twinkling toes on a banana slide.

Lizards leap, in shades so bright,
Dancing shadows in the golden light.
A pineapple falls with a splashy thud,
"Don't mind me!" it shouts from the mud.

Dancing partners, missteps collide,
"Oops! Sorry!" as they sail and glide.
The rhythm's wild, what a sight!
Belly laughs make the night feel right.

Bongo beats and tambourine chime,
Who knew this chaos was prime time?
A coconut drink spills like a waterfall,
But hey, who cares? We're having a ball!

Beneath Sapphire Skies

Sunshine giggles, clouds play peek,
A coconut grin; it's quite the cheek.
Sunglasses slip, a dog's warm bite,
Chasing shadows feels so right.

Kites soar high, getting tangled tight,
While waves crash down, what a sight!
Sandy costumes, slightly askew,
"Is that a mermaid, or just you?"

A tarpon thinks it's quite the show,
To splash and flick as we applaud below.
Tanned skin burns with laughter bright,
As sunscreen fights this glowing light!

So sing a tune beneath blue skies,
Catch the palm fronds as they rise.
Life's a party, let's all agree,
Under this sapphire jubilee!

Hushed Lullabies of the Tides

Moonlight whispers, gentle and sly,
As crabs scuttle beneath the sky.
Waves serenade with a salty hum,
While seashells giggle, 'Come! Have fun!'

Flip-flops flop on the boardwalk wide,
And starfish wink; they're full of pride.
A hammock sways with a sleepy sigh,
"Did I win the lottery?" says a nearby fly.

Fireflies blink like disco balls,
While sea turtles crawl, making calls.
Laughter floats in the soft sea foam,
Even the dolphins feel at home.

So hush your worries, let night unfurl,
Join in the laughter, let your heart twirl.
Under these stars, let's have a spin,
With whispers of joy—the night shall begin!

Driftwood Diaries

On a piece of wood so fine,
Crabs throw parties, oh divine!
They sip on seawater, dance with glee,
Even the seagulls join for free.

Palms sway with the ocean's beat,
Bikini-clad lizards tap their feet.
Each knot holds secrets, tales untold,
Of beach bum dreams and sun-soaked gold.

But wait! A flip-flop flies with flair,
Lands on a crab, a funny scare!
They tumble down, but none complain,
Just laugh it off, like it's a game.

Oh, driftwood diaries, tell us more,
Of sandy antics and ocean's roar.
Bring on the tales of the carefree kind,
Where the horizon meets a joyful mind.

Tropical Sunsets and Starry Skies

Sunsets dripping in pink and gold,
While the parrots squawk tales of old.
A fish jumps high, aiming for fame,
Splashing the tourists, what a game!

Stars twinkle like fireflies in flight,
As jellyfish glow with pure delight.
The night crickets play their tune,
Under the watchful gaze of the moon.

An octopus dons a top hat bold,
To woo a mermaid, it's been told.
As laughter echoes through the sea,
"Dance with me, with glee, with glee!"

What a sight, this twinkling show,
With all the creatures stealing the glow.
In this paradise, the fun won't cease,
Where every night is a crazy feast.

A Symphony of Rustling Leaves

Leaves rustle like giggling kids,
Play hide and seek around the bids.
With monkeys swinging branch to branch,
They flip and flop, what a wild dance!

A toucan's call is quite the laugh,
Echoing like a cheeky gaffe.
It steals a coconut like a thief,
And the jungle bustles with disbelief.

Squirrels chatter while the vines unwind,
Each twist and turn, a new find.
Sometimes a lizard plays a trick,
Dressing in colors, oh so slick!

From dawn till dusk, the jungle plays,
With humorous tunes and wild arrays.
In this leafy realm, joy is the tune,
As laughter rises beneath the moon.

Morning Dew on Hibiscus Petals

Morning dew on petals bright,
A lazy bee takes its flight.
It bumps the rose, oh what a fuss,
While the sun laughs, "What's the rush?"

Hibiscus dance with a fragrant sway,
As butterflies come to play.
A ladybug spins on a leaf,
While ants gossip about the chief.

Each petal holds a drop of cheer,
Tickling toes that wander near.
What fun it is to start the day,
With nature's jests in bright array!

So sip your coffee, smile wide,
With floral friends always beside.
In this garden where joy ignites,
Mirth blooms bright, in endless sights.

Lull of the Coral Sands

The crab in a hat does a dance,
Chasing shadows, taking a chance.
With a wiggle and a silly grin,
It's the funniest show you'll see, my friend!

Seagulls cackle, sharing a tale,
Of a fish that tried to set sail.
On a tiny board made of driftwood,
He paddled around thinking he could!

Sandy toes and the sun at play,
Makes the beach a humorous stay.
Watch the coconut fall from its throne,
Landing near you, but it's all in good fun!

So grab a towel, and join the cheer,
For laughter resonates when the coast is clear.
Under the sun where worries are few,
The beach is a circus just waiting for you.

Woven Dreams of Vivid Flora

In the garden where colors collide,
A parrot jokes, full of pride.
He squawks, 'Why did the flower rise?
To tickle the bees and claim the prize!'

Sunflowers peek, trying to see,
If the daisies are jelly at their spree.
Bumblebees buzz with a silly song,
'Our pollen party can't be wrong!'

Pineapples wear hats made of leaves,
While the orchids plot with the breeze.
Nature giggles as petals twirl,
In this zany, cartwheeling world.

So come unwind among blooms and cheer,
Where each bloom's a joker spreading good cheer.
In this garden where fun takes flight,
Even butterflies laugh at their own height!

Reflections in a Tropical Mirage

Mirages shimmer, playing tricks,
A lizard lounges, his clever mix.
Sipping sunshine from a fern,
Waiting to see the tides return!

Palm trees sway with a chuckle here,
As monkeys hoot without any fear.
One swings by with a splashy dive,
'I'm the king of the jungle, come alive!'

Figures dance in the golden mist,
A clam debates with a starfish, 'Just exist!'
Seashells whisper their secrets loud,
'Join the party, let's be proud!'

Echoes of laughter ripple the bay,
Where the sun and sea know how to play.
In this mirage, not all is as seems,
It's a land of whimsy, and bubble beams!

Caress of the Warm Trade Winds

The warm winds laugh, a playful tease,
Tickling faces, bending trees.
They sing a song of salty cheer,
As beach balls bounce, nothing to fear!

A whale splashes, causing a stir,
While surfboards wobble, making us purr.
'Take that wave, just don't fall flat!'
Says a seagull while looking all sprat!

Kids chase crabs like a wild parade,
Each one hiding in their sandy shade.
The horizon twirls, a kaleidoscope,
Wrapped in laughter and dreams like a rope.

So let the winds wrap you in glee,
As they whisper secrets from the sea.
With every gust, let joy transcend,
In this playful moment, let laughter blend!

Secrets in the Foliage

In the jungle, rumors spread,
Monkeys gossip, quite misled.
Parrots squawk of wild affairs,
While sloths nap in lazy chairs.

Lizards slide on leafy trails,
Whispering about fishy tales.
Squirrels steal each other's snacks,
And owls just roll their sleepy backs.

Bees buzz loudly, oh what fun,
Swapping secrets in the sun.
While frogs ribbit their own news,
In the breeze, there's much to lose.

Underneath the palm tree's shade,
Confessions made but never paid.
Echoes dance through vines and trees,
Life's a riddle on the breeze.

Whims of the Distant Horizon

The sun winks at the ocean's edge,
While crabs juggle on the ledge.
Seagulls squawk their silly tunes,
And fish flip flop under moons.

Coconut dreams float up with breeze,
As turtles tease the dancing leaves.
A parrot shrieks, "I was the best!"
Echoing the seagull's jest.

Smelly seaweed takes a bow,
As beach balls bounce, no one knows how.
The horizon giggles, takes a ride,
With silly waves that tangle and slide.

In the distance, a joke is spun,
As all the seashells laugh and run.
With every splash, a smile's born,
Under the rays of a new dawn.

Lovelorn Crickets at Dusk

As the sun dips low and life slows down,
Crickets sing their love-filled frown.
With tiny hearts that thrum like drums,
Dreaming of sweethearts, oh so dumb!

One croaks low, a verse of cheer,
While nearby bugs all stop to hear.
The moon rolls eyes, a lover's snare,
Tickling tunes float through the air.

Grasshoppers join in, quick and spry,
Making leaps while the stars get shy.
They chirp tales of romance and strife,
In twilight's glow, they flirt with life.

With every chirp and every laugh,
Nature's ballad writes a stanza half.
In this serenade, time stands still,
As dusk enwraps them with a thrill.

Temptations of the Soft Seafoam

Waves giggle, tickling shores,
While shells hide treasures, oh, what scores!
Sandcastles rise with puffs of glee,
As sea breezes dance wild and free.

The soft foam whispers to the sand,
"Build me castles, oh so grand!"
While crabs try hard to steal the show,
In their tiny suits, putting on a glow.

Mermaids wink from the ocean's blue,
Flipping hair, they know what to do.
Each wave a joke, a splash of mirth,
Floats mischievously, full of worth.

In the sun's warm embrace, they play,
Life's a beach with games all day.
With every tide, a giggle passed,
A seaside saga that holds steadfast.

Sighs of the Forgotten Isle

On a beach so far away,
A crab danced with dismay,
He slipped right on a shell,
And tumbled like a spell.

The seagulls laughed in glee,
As waves rolled out for tea,
The sun wore shades, so bright,
While coconuts took flight.

A parrot shared a tale,
Of a turtle with a sail,
He couldn't quite get far,
But made it to the bar.

The palm trees sway and sway,
Saying "Let's go out and play!"
But instead of beachy fun,
They shaded everyone!

The Story of the Wandering Tides.

There once were tides so sly,
They'd sneak and wink, oh my!
Dancing with the moonlight,
And playing peek-a-boo at night.

Fish wearing party hats,
Joined in with joyful chats,
They splashed about so bold,
Singing songs of old.

But oh, a wave turned round,
And dropped its foam on ground,
The beachgoers all shrieked,
As they ran away, quite freaked!

In between the dips and dives,
The water jived and jives,
With laughter, joy, and fun,
Their party never done!

Whispers of the Ocean Breeze

A breeze whizzed by with flair,
Tickling toes and salty hair,
"Tide's in," it chimed with cheer,
And dolphins joined in, oh dear!

Shells wore mismatched outfits bright,
Inviting crabs to dance in flight,
A conch shell shared a joke,
As waves of laughter woke.

The sunbeams tried to steal the show,
But shadows played a game below,
With giggles echoing near,
The sea felt full of cheer.

As stars began to peek,
The ocean let out a squeak,
With whispers oh-so-fine,
It's a party every time!

Secrets Beneath the Coconut Palms

Under palms so lush and green,
Squirrels plotted quite a scene,
With coconuts for chairs,
They played hide-and-seek with stares.

A breezy gossip spread so fast,
About the sloth who ran at last,
He dashed to grab a snack,
But ended up on his back.

The crickets chirped a tune so sweet,
Enticing slugs to tap their feet,
A dance-off ensued, oh dear,
With coconuts all cheering loud and clear!

As the sun dipped low and shy,
The night lit up a twinkling sky,
Secrets swayed in every breeze,
Beneath the palms and swaying leaves.

Wistful Glances Beyond the Palm Trees

Beneath the sunny skies, we roam,
With flip-flops flying, we call this home.
The crabs dance sideways, quite a sight,
While seagulls squawk about taking flight.

Sipping coconut juice, all aglow,
Our sunburns tell tales of summer's show.
The sand sticks stubbornly to our toes,
While gossiping waves trade jellyfish woes.

In hammocks we swing, lazy and free,
Plotting out schemes for a grand banana spree.
The sunset paints laughter across our face,
As we toss our worries into the waves' embrace.

Each breeze brings whispers of laughter so bright,
Join in the fun, it feels just right.
With each kooky flip on the beach we make,
We're all just kids, it's the joy we take.

A World Wrapped in Soft Light

In a glow of dusk, we twirl and sway,
Our shadowy sillhouettes dance and play.
The fireflies flicker, a light show grand,
While we trip on roots from the nearby land.

With laughter bubbling like mango lemonade,
A parade of thoughts where dreams are laid.
The breeze is a tickle, we can't keep still,
As sparrows join in, chasing after a thrill.

The evening whispers quirky tales to the night,
While we munch on chips, staring at starlight.
Chasing tall drinks with colorful straws,
Toasting to life with unworthy applause.

The moon grins down on our silly spree,
Sudden clowning is always the key.
As we giggle and grin, wrapped in delight,
We're just a bunch of oddballs, high on the night!

The Heartbeat of the Living Shore

Where laughter meets the ocean's roar,
We practice our diving, but mostly just floor.
With flippers on backwards, we wobble about,
Like fish out of water, we giggle and shout.

Surfers in sunglasses, wave riders bold,
Telling tall tales of the waves they've sold.
But the tides just chuckle, keeping their score,
As we wipe out again, back to the shore.

Shells hold our secrets of days gone by,
With seaweed crowned kings, they rule from high.
Sardines throw parties, they jive on parade,
While we join their dance, in laughter we wade.

With sunscreen as war paint, we battle the sun,
Chasing the crabs, 'til our day is done.
For in this little world, we bravely explore,
The heartbeat of laughter spills out on the shore.

Horizons Beneath Whispering Stars

The stars twinkle bright, a cosmic way,
   Fishes swim by, having their play.
A crab in a tux, with a pinch and a grin,
   Dances on sand, let the laughter begin.

A parrot screams jokes, a stand-up delight,
   While dolphins do flips in the moonlight.
A hammock reclines, but it's fallen askew,
   The coconut laughs, at the chaos it drew.

In the laughter of waves, the night takes a bow,
   The seaweed's a wig, who needs a hair vow?
Each splash pushes hard for a comedic burst,
   Underneath the stars, with fun as our thirst.

As friends all unite on this beach so absurd,
   We're living our best with every silly word.
So raise up your drinks, let's hear the waves play,
   Where humor meets horizons in a cheeky ballet.

Laughter Beneath the Canopy

Beneath leafy arches, the monkeys convene,
Juggling ripe bananas, oh what a scene!
A toucan in shades sips his juice with a flair,
While sloths tell their jokes without a hurry or care.

The lizards are laughing, they take center stage,
With antics so silly, they deserve a live gauge.
A squirrel in a tutu leaps up on a vine,
The audience cheers with a round of "divine!"

While rain drips like giggles, tan lines make a mark,
We dance to the rhythm, our spirits embark.
Nature's wild laughter, a grand comedy show,
In a world so absurd, let's take it real slow!

From patterned capes to funny little pranks,
Every twist and turn, we give thanks and give thanks.
In the shade of the trees, where humor runs free,
We find joy in the jungle, just you wait and see.

The Aroma of Ocean Blooms

In the air, the fragrance of a wild coconut,
Brings smiles and giggles, it's never a rut.
Seaweed and flowers mix up a fine brew,
While sea cucumbers crack up, with their sight of blue.

An octopus chef with eight forks on a plate,
Serves snacks that are silly, oh isn't that great?
Each wave that rolls in, tells a pun so grand,
With salt in the breeze, life's humor is planned.

From fish in a fedora to turtles in suits,
Every giddy creature gets into its roots.
The blossoms are laughing, their petals do sway,
Creating aromas that dance and play.

As we gather the smiles on this flavorful shore,
With scents and with laughter, who could ask for more?
Let's feast on the fun as we surf through the blooms,
In a banquet of mischief that joyfully looms.

Serenities in the Swaying Palms

Under swaying palms, the breeze tells a tale,
Of crabs wearing hats, and a snail with a sail.
The sun winks cheekily, rays tickling the ground,
Where laughter bubbles up in a silly surround.

A parrot steals snacks from a beachcomber's pack,
While flip-flops do tango, a dance with a knack.
A piña colada sings, with a twisty little rhyme,
As the sand squeaks softly, keeping meter and time.

The waves clap in rhythm, not wanting to drown,
While clouds share their puns, oh you silly ol' clown!
Let's twirl 'round the island, no worries in sight,
For every warm chuckle, keeps our spirits alight.

So join in the madness, don't be afraid,
The mirth in the palms is serenely displayed.
As we sway with the breeze, let the joy be our guide,
In this land of the silly, where laughter's our pride.

Mosaics of Coastal Serenity

Beneath the palm, the crab takes a stroll,
His sideways dance makes us lose control.
The seagulls laugh as they swoop and dive,
While we try to eat without making a mess alive.

The waves tickle toes, oh what a delight,
A splash here, a giggle, as we try to take flight.
A coconut falls with a thud, not a cheer,
We duck for cover, our laughter we hear.

Sandcastles rise as the tide rolls out,
With moats of giggles, we're filled with a shout.
A lost flip-flop floats far out to sea,
"Hey! That's my shoe!" shrieks the child with glee.

Under the sun, where fun never ends,
We toast with drinks, as the light bends.
Let's dance with the lizards, oh what a sight,
They scamper away with our snack, in the night.

The Song of Wandering Spirits

An echoing laugh from a parrot's beak,
Calls out our names, oh, what a freak!
The waves whisper secrets in bubbly foam,
They tease us gently, away from home.

Ghost crabs host parties in the glowing sand,
With tiny top hats, they've got a fine band.
A conch shell trumpet blares a tune,
As we join in the dance beneath the moon.

The spirits of shells chatter and tease,
Tickling our toes with a playful breeze.
"Join the fiesta!" they chant with a grin,
We slip and we slide, let the antics begin!

With colorful fish wearing hats so grand,
We laugh at the tales in this magical land.
For laughter's the key, as the sun sinks low,
In this realm of whispers, we steal the show.

Revelations of Fleeting Sunsets

The sun melts like butter on warm toast,
Creating colors that we love the most.
As we munch on chips, the sky turns bright,
"Is it dinner time?" we squeal in delight.

A dancing dolphin leaps, what a sight!
It throws us confetti, all sparkly and light.
We try to catch rays, like old pros we pose,
But the fish just giggle, with their wiggly toes.

In dripping ice cream, we make silly faces,
While the horizon blushes in its playful embraces.
The waves dress in orange, a bright candy swirl,
As we sing off-key, letting our dreams twirl.

Each sunset's a canvas, where laughter ignites,
Turning moments to magic, in soft, silly flights.
So we toast to the sky, with spritzers in hand,
For each fleeting glow, we've made our own band.

Tides of Joy in a Sea-Shell's Heart

In a shell's embrace, where secrets are kept,
Lies a choir of whispers that laugh as we stepped.
With each crashing wave, a giggle we find,
"Are you hearing this?" we ask, quite blind.

Seashells hold treasures, but mostly just sand,
We search for the shiny ones, oh so grand!
But the biggest surprise? A crab in a hat,
Gives us a wink, then scuttles off flat.

With laughter like bubbles in fresh ocean air,
We twirl in our flip-flops without a care.
The tide pulls us in like a game of tag,
And we squeal with joy as we run with a brag.

As dolphins debate if they'll join the parade,
We sit with our snacks, that fun never fades.
For every shell whispers a laugh from the sea,
Where joy tides in laughter, forever carefree.

Shadow Play of Palm Fronds

Beneath the palms, a shadow prances,
A playful dance that never glances.
Chasing crabs with wiggly legs,
They tumble, giggle, like silly pegs.

Laughter echoes, like a song,
Even the coconuts join along.
Feet in the sand, oh what a jest,
As waves come knocking, they jest the best.

Fronds in the breeze tell goofy tales,
Of funny fish with let-out sails.
While birds up high in zany flight,
Double-dare the sun to shine too bright.

The sunset smirks, its colors gleam,
And calls us back, it's all a dream.
As shadows stretch and beams confide,
The night-time laughs at the day's pride.

The Language of the Wet Earth

Rain drops tap like a drummer's beat,
Water's laughter is oh-so-sweet.
Worms in tuxedos slide with flair,
While mushrooms puff out in fresh air.

Puddles splatter with giggly glee,
Making frogs feel like royalty.
A dance-off starts with soggy shoes,
As leaves gossip about the news.

The earth speaks softly, muddy and bright,
With worms crafting jokes late at night.
Each droplet hiccups, a funny show,
As flowers sway in the ebb and flow.

Mossy cushions and dampened cheer,
Unfurling the laughs the soil holds dear.
A wet parade on squishy streets,
Where giggles bounce in rhythmic beats.

Colors of an Island Sunset

The sun slips down, a clown in flight,
Painting the sky with hues so bright.
Pinks and oranges swirl like ice,
While seagulls laugh, oh, what a slice!

Banana boats bob with silly grace,
As waves roll in, they join the race.
Sunset smoothies in a peachy cup,
With every sip, we just can't stop!

Clouds wear shades like hipsters pretend,
Having fun until the day's end.
A coconut whispers, "Just take a sip,"
While the surf chants out a funny tip.

As colors blend, the island grins,
Throwing a party, oh, where it begins?
With laughter swirling in the twilight time,
Even the crickets start to rhyme.

Veranda Dreams under Star-Kissed Skies

On the veranda, dreams take flight,
As fireflies dance in the soft twilight.
Laughter spills from every chair,
While shadows play without a care.

The stars above winkle with glee,
As we share jokes about a bee.
Each sip of drink, a fizzy cheer,
"Why did you come?" the stars all jeer!

A hammock sways, a gentle tease,
The moon giggles, it's quite the breeze.
Tickles of night with a light embrace,
As we dream fun in this magical place.

Chasing the night with a silly grin,
Our hearts and laughter like a whirlwind.
Under star-kissed skies, let's stay awhile,
In dreams of joy, let's make them smile.

www.ingramcontent.com/pod-product-compliance
Lightning Source LLC
Chambersburg PA
CBHW072216070526
44585CB00015B/1365